DISCARD

Published by Creative Education
123 South Broad Street, Mankato, Minnesota 56001
Creative Education is an imprint of The Creative Company

Designed by Stephanie Blumenthal
Production Design by The Design Lab

Photos by: Allsport, Archive Photos, Sportschrome, and Vantage Point.

Copyright © 2000 Creative Education.
International copyrights reserved in all countries.
No part of this book may be reproduced in any form without
written permission from the publisher.

Library of Congress Cataloging-in-Publication Data

Frisch, Aaron, 1975–
Eric Lindros / by Aaron Frisch
p. cm. — (Ovations)
Summary: A biography of the man who won the National Hockey
League's Most Valuable Player award and captained the Philadelphia
Flyers to their first Stanley Cup appearance in a decade.
ISBN 0-88682-998-4

1. Lindros, Eric—Juvenile literature. 2. Hockey players—Canada—
Biography—Juvenile literature. [1. Lindros, Eric. 2. Hockey players.]
I. Title. II. Series: Ovations (Mankato, Minn.)

GV848.5.L56F75   1999
796.962'092—dc21
[B]   98-33684

First edition

2 4 6 8 9 7 5 3 1

OVATIONS

ERIC

LINDROS

BY AARON FRISCH

Creative Education

REFLECTIONS

Standing a broad-shouldered 6-foot-4 and weighing 236 pounds, Eric Lindros is a tower of strength. His size makes him intimidating, but it is his seemingly dual personality that makes him so intriguing.

On the ice, he is a ferocious hockey player with a slap shot like a cannon blast. Dressed in the black and orange colors of the Philadelphia Flyers, Eric flies across the ice like a tiger, crushing opposing players with bone-breaking body checks and firing screaming shots past bewildered goalies. As one opponent summed up, "Guys are scared to play against him."

But off the ice, when he changes from hockey pads to blue jeans, Eric becomes a soft-spoken young man. During post-game interviews, he removes himself from the

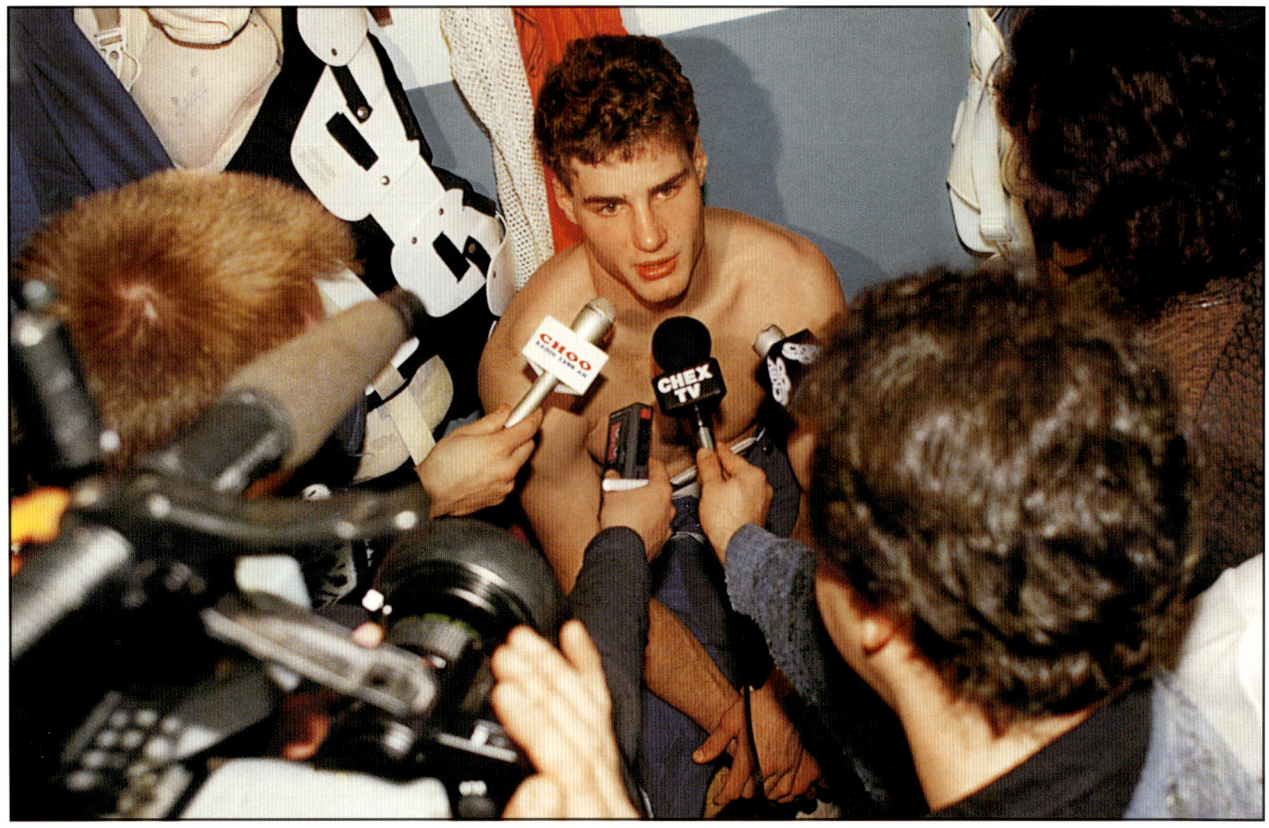

spotlight and humbly emphasizes his teammates' roles in the Flyers' win. He spends time at children's hospitals, brightening the days of some of his biggest fans. He is the type of person you might bump into at the grocery store.

As nearly every fan of the sport agrees, Eric is the greatest hockey player on earth. This is the way it was supposed to be. Eric's hockey success during his teenage years is legendary. By the time he was 15, hockey fans around the world had heard of the coming of "The Next One."

Although the pressure placed on him has been enormous, Eric has met all expectations—and more. His clean-cut way of life has made him a positive role model for the thousands of kids who wear his number 88 jersey. He has won the National Hockey League's Most Valuable Player award. He has captured the hearts of a city by leading the Flyers to their first Stanley Cup appearance in a decade. He also has yet to reach his prime.

Although he has always been hounded by the media in the locker room and public places, Eric prefers to let his on-ice dominance do most of the talking.

EVOLUTION

Eric Bryan Lindros seemed destined for athletic greatness from his birth in London, Ontario, on February 28, 1973. His father Carl had spent time playing both professional hockey and football, and his mother Bonnie was a former track star. The sports-minded couple soon steered their young son toward that greatest of Canadian pastimes: hockey.

Flooding the backyard into a skating rink in the winter, Carl taught Eric to skate by the age of four. Eric was soon knocking a hockey puck around the rink, where he and his younger brother Brett spent many winter nights.

When Eric started playing league hockey with other children at the age of six, it was obvious that he was special. "Eric had an understanding of the game," his father said. "He

would be doing something, and you would be scratching your head wondering what he was up to, but the puck would end up being there."

For the next several years, Eric continued to amaze onlookers with his skill and instinct for the game. He also impressed people with his humility. As he took home virtually every league award at the age of 10, Eric insisted that he share the scoring title with a teammate, without whom, he said, he could not have scored so much.

Although hockey came easily to Eric, making friends did not. Big for his age, he was a shy and self-conscious loner. His social awkwardness made him the target of older bullies, and he earned some bruises early in life defending himself. When Eric was on the ice, he was confident and aggressive. But away from hockey, he was a quiet kid who, as his mother Bonnie recalled, was so sensitive that he would sometimes cry as she read "Lassie Come Home" to him.

Even into his teens, Eric struggled to fit in socially. He was often laughed at by his peers, who called him "grampa" because he always seemed so careful of what he said or did. Such ridicule drew Eric more and more into hockey, and he continued to grow more unstoppable.

When Eric was 15, the Lindros family, including Eric's younger sister

Although Eric moved from one hockey organization to the next as a teenager, he could always rely on the constant support and encouragement of his family.

Robin, moved to Toronto. There Eric immediately dominated on the St. Michael's Junior B Buzzers, a widely known youth hockey program. As his supportive parents watched from the stands at every game, Eric ran wild, steamrolling 21-year-old players and averaging almost two points per game.

Hockey experts around the country had taken notice of Eric; his name began to appear in sports headlines throughout Canada and even in the United States and Europe. He wasn't even old enough to drive, and already sportswriters were beginning to call him "The Next One," the hockey player who was destined to someday replace Wayne Gretzky as the world's greatest.

When he turned 16, Eric received the most prized possession of his young life: a stick signed by Mark Messier, a tough NHL center whom Eric idolized. That birthday also made him eligible for Ontario's junior draft. When the Sault Ste. Marie Greyhounds were awarded the first pick, Eric and his parents told the Greyhounds that Eric would not play there; Sault Ste. Marie was too far from home, and Carl and Bonnie feared that Eric's education would suffer.

When the Greyhounds selected him with the first pick anyway, Eric refused to join the team. Instead, he finished high school while playing for a junior team near Detroit, Michigan. The Greyhounds, who had retained league rights to Eric, finally traded him to the Oshawa Generals, a team closer to Toronto.

Eric's reputation continued to grow as he helped Canada win two junior world championships. He also helped the Oshawa Generals claim the Memorial Cup as league champions and took home virtually every award in the league. As Eric neared his 18th birthday and closed out his junior career as Canada's all-time leading scorer in world junior play, NHL scouts were nearly frantic with anticipation. Every team in the league wanted "The Package," the kid who combined the size, strength, speed, and skills to become the league's best player in decades—perhaps ever.

Taking Center Ice

The city of Quebec rejoiced when the Quebec Nordiques were awarded the first pick in the 1991 NHL entry draft. Cries of happiness soon turned to cries of outrage, however, when Eric announced that he would not play for the Nordiques. He felt that the team's management treated players poorly, the team was lousy, and the city was too small to offer many off-ice opportunities.

Quebec drafted Eric anyway and tried to change his mind with a 10-year, $55 million contract. When he still said no, Eric instantly became a villain in Quebec. It was the second time he had refused the team that had drafted him, and the media blasted Eric and his parents.

"It was the best thing I ever did," Eric said. To him, being happy playing somewhere else was more valuable than the millions of dollars waved at him in Quebec. "[The Nordiques' owner] told me that if I went to Quebec, I'd be a god. To be quite honest with you, I don't care to be a god."

Eric's unrivaled success as a teenager in Ontario's junior league gave hockey fans an early glimpse at one of the most explosive players of all time.

As the media backlash continued, Eric took a year off from steady hockey. He continued to make headlines as he played against grown men for the first time in his life in the 1991 Canada Cup, an international tournament. In one game, the 18-year-old holdout drew a bead on Ulf Samuelsson, one of the NHL's heavy hitters, and belted him with a monstrous check that separated the veteran's shoulder. Two nights later, after a Lindros hit broke another player's collarbone, opponents gave Eric a wide berth, and Canada didn't lose another game.

Eric also won a silver medal on Canada's 1992 Olympic team before the Nordiques reluctantly sent him to the Philadelphia Flyers in the biggest trade in NHL history. Pierre Pagé, the Nordiques' general manager who drafted Eric, could only shake his head sadly. "We knew this guy was going to be the best player in the NHL," he said. "He had skill, toughness—everything in one package. Six players, two first-round draft picks, and $15 million. And the trade still wasn't even. That's how good Eric Lindros is."

Eric's first year in the NHL was a tough one. *New York Times* magazine placed him on its cover with the headline, "Can This Man Save Hockey?" Only 19 years old, he had to adjust to living by himself for the first time in a strange city. As Eric dealt with the pressure and feelings of loneliness, he also had to face choruses of boos from fans around the league who interpreted his holdout in Quebec as snobbishness.

On the ice, Eric proved that he was worth everything the Flyers had traded for him. Opponents learned the hard way to avoid contact with big number 88, and teammates quickly came to respect him for his unselfish play. The fans of Philadelphia—who are notoriously hard to please—were instantly captivated by their powerful young center.

Unfortunately, the same aggressive play that made Eric the league's fastest rising star also led to injuries and a lot of penalty minutes during his first season. Knee injuries forced Eric to miss 23 games. But when he was on the ice, Eric was always willing to drop his gloves and fight any challenger. Although his awesome strength nearly always made him victorious, the Flyers were the real losers as he skated away to the penalty box.

Eric continued to amaze people in his second year. No one had ever seen such a powerful man with such

After leading Canada to gold in the 1991 junior world championship, Eric donned the black and orange of the Philadelphia Flyers and became an instant force in the NHL.

agility. Often he would take control of the puck and bull-rush the net, easily knocking large defenders aside or driving them helplessly backward. Other times, as opponents would brace themselves for Eric's brute strength, he might slip the puck between their skates, side-step them, regain the puck, and backhand it into the top corner of the net.

Eric's incredible power and aggressiveness prompted some teams around the league to call him a brutal and intentionally vicious player. Eric, however, laughed at the accusation. "I wouldn't term myself as brutal," he said. "It's all part of hockey."

This physical approach quickly returned a certain toughness to a franchise once known as the "Broad Street Bullies" for its intimidating style of play during the mid-1970s. Bobby Clarke, who captained the fearsome Bullies and is now the Flyers' general manager, has seen that same pride resurface in Philadelphia. "I can feel the people of this city pulling for Eric Lindros the same way they did the old Broad Street Bullies," Clarke said.

An impressive second season, in which Eric racked up 44 goals and 53 assists, was marred by his brother Brett's forced retirement from hockey. Although he had played only 51 games after making it into the NHL, Brett

After watching his brother Brett, bottom, forced from pro hockey by injuries, Eric continued to bully the opposition and was soon named captain of the intimidating Flyers.

had suffered too many concussions to continue playing. Eric broke down in tears as his brother made the announcement.

Eric began his third season as the NHL's youngest team captain. "This is definitely Eric Lindros's team," Flyers coach Terry Murray said. "The team takes on his personality. Everybody watches him and takes his lead." Flyers management made it clear that they wanted it to be Eric's team by lining up John LeClair and Mikael Renberg—two big, fast wings—alongside him. Together, the hard-hitting trio became known as the "Legion of Doom," the most dreaded line in hockey.

With his bruising new linemates helping him to prowl the ice, Eric had a career season in 1994–95, winning the Hart Trophy for the NHL's Most Valuable Player and leading the Flyers to the Atlantic Division crown. A scary eye injury near the end of the season cost him an almost-certain Art Ross Trophy, given to the league's highest goal scorer. The injury also left Eric at less than full strength in the ensuing playoffs, and the Flyers lost in the conference finals.

At a ceremony after the playoffs, intense feelings of relief washed over Eric as he was handed the Hart Trophy. He became choked up as he thanked the Flyers' fans who had stuck with the team through the bad years. After the ceremony, though, a playful Eric denied his near-miss with tears, claiming, "I didn't cry. I was about to sneeze. I had this itch. . . ."

A BIG-HEARTED BRUISER

Perhaps the most amazing thing about Eric is not his incredible achievements at such a young age, but the fact that success hasn't spoiled him. Although he is the sport's premier star, he remains one of its most modest. During post-game interviews, he prefers to talk about the team, rarely commenting at length on his own play.

And while his success, good looks, and down-to-earth personality make Eric the obvious choice as the NHL's spokesman, it is not a role he wants to carry alone. "It can't be just one or two guys that carry the whole league," he said. "[W]e can get a lot more accomplished by spreading it out and giving everybody the light." Eric also has insisted that all Flyers promotional activities involve as many team members as possible. This unselfishness has earned Eric the respect of players throughout the league.

He may be a tiger on skates when he hits the ice, but Eric has always been a quiet and introspective young man who values his private time away from hockey.

He makes millions of dollars, but money has never driven Eric. He has been offered many rich endorsement opportunities and has turned almost all of them down. After the 1997 season, when it came time to renew his contract, Eric made it clear that he wanted to stay with the Flyers, even if it cost him millions of dollars to do so. In an era when many professional athletes hold out for every possible penny and then say, "It's not about the money," Eric has let his actions prove his priorities.

Never one to flash his wealth with material possessions, Eric wears blue jeans and drives a Chevy pickup. Single, he lives alone with Bacchus, his Great Dane, at his house in Voorhees, New Jersey. His hobbies are simple and laid-back: working on home-improvement projects, cooking, golfing, and fishing and hiking at his secluded cabin on a lake in Canada.

He says he is happiest just hanging out with teammates in the locker room or retreating to the backyard rink of his childhood home.

Eric also uses his time, money, and fame to help the less fortunate. Although he is a very private person who never publicizes his generous actions, those close to him know his kindness. He spends many free afternoons in children's hospitals and promotes Flyers charity events to raise money for the Children's Miracle Network in the Philadelphia area.

In spite of his reputation as the most feared man in hockey, Eric is quite good with kids. Visiting with one boy who had to wear a hockey-style helmet after a head injury, Eric signed a picture to him: "Your helmet looks great. Keep wearing it. I wear mine. All the best, Eric Lindros." After Eric left, the boy said he was never shaking anyone else's hand again. "I walk away from these visits feeling like a million bucks," Eric said.

SHOOTING FOR THE TOP

After suffering another loss in the second round of the 1996 playoffs, Eric grew into a smarter player and a more confident leader in 1996–97. In an unforgettable playoff stretch, he seized the torch as the NHL's new king by knocking off several active hockey legends.

His intense approach and knack for scoring have made Eric the NHL's most powerful player, a title he commandeered from such hockey greats as Mario Lemieux, opposite top, and Wayne Gretzky (left) and Mark Messier (right), opposite bottom.

The first round of the playoffs pitted the Flyers against the Pittsburgh Penguins, and Eric against Mario Lemieux, one of the greatest players of the modern era. Five games later, a beaten Lemieux pulled Eric aside. "I told him it was his time," Lemieux said. "That team can win the Stanley Cup."

After rolling over the Buffalo Sabres in the second round, the Flyers faced the powerful New York Rangers in the Eastern Conference Finals. Fans prepared to watch an epic battle, not only between two of the NHL's most bitter rivals, but between Eric and two of the league's reigning kings—"The Great One," Wayne Gretzky, and Mark Messier, the fearless center Eric idolized as a kid.

Temporarily setting aside respect for his elders, Eric pummeled the veteran Rangers. Three Lindros assists and intense bodychecking led to a game one Flyers' win. In game three, Eric scored three goals—recording his first career playoff hat trick—and left Messier looking small and breathless along the way. After Eric's last-second backhand shot won game four, the

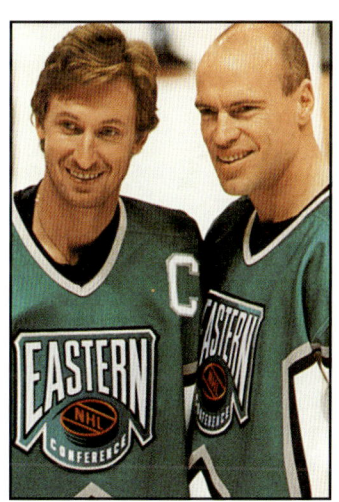

Flyers returned to CoreStates Arena in Philadelphia to put the reeling Rangers out of their misery in front of the elated Flyers fans.

Although the Flyers struggled and were swept in four games in the Stanley Cup Finals by the Detroit Red Wings, Eric knew that his team was on the doorstep to winning it all.

Midway through the 1997–98 season, Eric's status in hockey was made clear to the world when he was awarded the prestigious position of captain of Canada's 1998 Olympic hockey team, a role he had dreamt about since childhood. After leading the country of his birth to a 4–2 record in Japan, Eric returned to Philadelphia to lead his team to a 42–29 regular-season finish. Unfortunately, the Flyers—who had been early-season favorites to return to the Stanley Cup Finals—saw their season end with a disappointing first-round playoff upset.

Although some critics have publicly wondered if Eric will ever capture the Stanley Cup, he remains confident in himself and in his team. The expectations of others have never weighed Eric down. "The ones I care to fulfill are the ones I have for myself," he said. As Eric continues to shoot for his own expectations, The Next One will undoubtedly leave an everlasting mark on the world of sports.

In a span of less than a year, a more mature Eric led the revitalized Flyers to the Stanley Cup Finals and captained Canada's hockey team in the 1998 Olympic Games.

V O I C E S

ON HIS IMPACT ON THE GAME:

"He's his own player and has a style that's different from anyone who's ever played the game, because of his size and speed. He possesses a lot more talent than I had at his age. He's a superstar of superstars."
Mark Messier, NHL center

"There's no one else in the league who's capable of scoring 50 goals and using you as a speed bump."
Shawn Antoski, NHL wing

"When Eric Lindros comes off the Flyers' bench against us, I shake—every time. That doesn't happen with anyone else."
Doug MacLean, NHL coach

"It's almost unfair. There's no one who can physically challenge him. He's so big and strong and skilled, he can hurt you in so many ways. Punch him in the head, [and] he might skate away and score on the power play. Or punch him in the head, [and] he might turn around and knock you out. For the next 10 or 12 years, he's the guy who's going to get you hooked on hockey."

   Ron Hextall, NHL goalie

"There is nobody more powerful in this league. I think we're just beginning to see what he's going to be . . . and he's already the most dominant player in the game."

   Jacques Demers, NHL coach

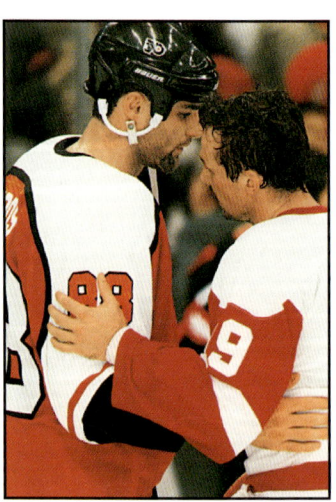

ON HIS POWER:

"He's the Darth Vader of hockey. I have seen him overpower three guys on the same play and still have enough strength to beat the goaltender. He's untouchable."

    Pierre Pagé, NHL coach

"He is like a train coming toward you. He just gets bigger and bigger, and then he hits you. Unfortunately, he is still on his feet, while I have to crawl back to the bench."

    Ray Bourque, NHL defenseman

"I would have chipped in a little of my salary if I had known there was a way to keep him out of our division. I can show you some welts I got from him in the conference finals last year that still haven't gone away."

    Scott Stevens, NHL defenseman

"I don't jump in and out of the play, trying to avoid contact. I can't play like that. The more . . . I wade into the thick of things, the better I play."

    Eric Lindros

"You find yourself watching him even when he doesn't have the puck, because you know at any time that coiled cobra can unleash."

    Bill Clement
    ESPN hockey analyst

Eric's aggressive play, towering stature, and willingness to fight any adversary have returned a "Broad Street Bullies" mentality to Philadelphia, leaving opponents grasping for ways to stop him.

On his leadership and maturity:

"He is a leader by example. And off the ice, you have to be a good guy and care about what goes on with the team."

*Dale Hawerchuk,
former NHL center*

"He provides the kind of leadership you hear about when people talk about Mark Messier. You know, the kind that you listen to—or else."

*Terry Murray,
former Flyers coach*

"The big guy has made the difference. Eric has learned how to use his size so that he's an intimidating presence every time he's on the ice. With experience, he's grown smarter. . . . He hits when the effect is greatest. He's definitely grown up—and ready to win a Stanley Cup."

*Bobby Clarke,
Flyers general manager*

"Being captain comes naturally in a way, because it's . . . showing the desire to win, doing what you can to get the other guys going. No big deal."

Eric Lindros

Four inches taller and 40 pounds heavier than the average NHL player, Eric's combination of speed, strength, agility, and fearlessness have made him one of the league's biggest attractions.

On the effects of money and fame:

"I'm a pretty simple guy, actually. I'm wearing the same pair of jeans I bought six years ago. . . . The money and recognition change some aspects of your life, but it's not like you change who you are. I'm content with the style of life I've chosen. It's real—it's me. Why go the other road, where people try to change the way you are?"

Eric Lindros

"I haven't changed. I hop in my pickup truck and go home after games and practices. And I still room with my brother when I go home to Toronto in the off-season."

Eric Lindros

On publicity:

"Eric's not somebody who wants to be more famous."

Brett Lindros

"I value my time away from the rink. I'm just a homebody. During the summer, I don't really aspire to go out and ring up endorsements all over the place. In the off-season, I'd rather just sit in my cottage and be with my friends and my family and play golf and fish. . . ."

Eric Lindros

Through his astounding offensive skills, spectacular hits, and devotion to the Flyers organization, Eric has earned the rousing support of the Philadelphia faithful.

"Wayne Gretzky sold hockey to southern California, and Eric Lindros could sell it to North America."

Leigh Steinberg, sports agent

ON THE VALUE OF HELPING OTHERS:

"I'd rather go about it quietly.... I think it's important to make contributions, but self-promotion through charity is not worth it."

Eric Lindros

"You can do a lot of good things with fame. You can reach a lot of people if you do it properly.... There are a lot of unfortunate people out there. What you do might not seem like a whole lot, but they see it differently. That hour or two at a hospital means a lot to those kids.... You feel good about yourself leaving.... And it makes you think about how fortunate we are."

Eric Lindros

"Once in a while there might be a small request, which is fine. It takes you a minute and a half to do and hopefully it makes a kid happy."

Eric Lindros

With the Flyers soaring high in the Eastern Conference behind the play of Eric and the talented John LeClair, bottom, it appears that the new millennium belongs to The Next One.

OVATIONS